DEC   2012

D1129596

ALABAMA
CRIMSON TIDE

BY JEFF SEIDEL

Published by ABDO Publishing Company, PO Box 398166, Minneapolis, MN 55439. Copyright © 2013 by Abdo Consulting Group, Inc. International copyrights reserved in all countries. No part of this book may be reproduced in any form without written permission from the publisher. SportsZone™ is a trademark and logo of ABDO Publishing Company.

Printed in the United States of America,
North Mankato, Minnesota
052012
092012

Editor: Chrös McDougall
Series Designer: Craig Hinton

Photo Credits: Dave Martin/AP Images, cover, 4, 12, 36, 41, 42 (bottom), 43 (bottom right); Focus on Sport/Getty Images, 1; Butch Dill/AP Images, 7, 43 (bottom left); Tom Hauck/AP Images, 9, 10; AP Images, 14, 20, 26, 29, 31, 42 (top left), 42 (top right), 43 (top); Robert Walsh/AP Images, 17; Horace Cort/AP Images, 18; Alabama/Collegiate Images/Getty Images, 22; Jim Cox, Houston Chronicle/AP Images, 25; Ronald C. Modra/Sports Imagery/Getty Images, 33; Allen Steele/Getty Images, 34; Kyle Carter, The Meridian Star/AP Images, 38; Dusty Compton, The Tuscaloosa News/AP Images, 44

Library of Congress Cataloging-in-Publication Data
Seidel, Jeff.
 Alabama Crimson Tide / by Jeff Seidel.
   p. cm. -- (Inside college football)
 Includes index.
 ISBN 978-1-61783-494-3
 1. University of Alabama--Football--History--Juvenile literature. 2. Alabama Crimson Tide (Football team)--History--Juvenile literature. I. Title.
 GV958.U513S45 2013
 796.332'630976184--dc23
                          2012001847

TABLE OF CONTENTS

DEC 2012

Alabama star running back Mark Ingram helped turn the Crimson Tide back into a national power.

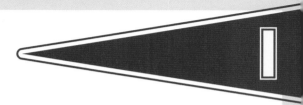

CHAMPIONS AGAIN

THE FOOTBALL PROGRAM AT THE UNIVERSITY OF
ALABAMA IS ONE OF THE NATION'S MOST SUCCESSFUL.
THROUGH 2011, THE CRIMSON TIDE HAVE WON 14 NATIONAL
CHAMPIONSHIPS AND PRODUCED SOME OF THE BEST-KNOWN
PLAYERS AND COACHES IN THE COUNTRY. THEY ALSO ARE
SUPPORTED BY AN INCREDIBLE FAN BASE.

The program went through a down period between its twelfth and thirteenth titles, though. Coach Gene Stallings guided Alabama to its twelfth title in 1992. Then the Crimson Tide struggled. Four coaches came and went from 1996 to 2006. None were able to bring much success.

The program ran into trouble off the field as well. In 2002, the National Collegiate Athletic Association (NCAA) punished Alabama for various recruiting violations. The NCAA even considered eliminating the program for a period of time.

"They were absolutely staring down the barrel of a gun," an NCAA official said. "These violations are some of the worst, most serious that have ever occurred."

The once-proud program seemed to be sinking. Coach Mike Shula took over in 2003. He was generally popular among fans. However, the Crimson Tide were not contending for national titles under him. In four seasons, Shula led the Tide to a 26–23 record. So athletic director Mal Moore decided to replace him after the 2006 season.

Alabama needed a good coach to turn things around. It found that coach in Nick Saban. He was coaching the Miami Dolphins in the National Football League (NFL) at the time. However, he had previously been a successful college coach at Toledo, Michigan State, and Louisiana State University (LSU). In fact, he had guided LSU to the 2003 national championship.

Some people were mad at Saban for accepting the job at Alabama. They felt he had turned his back on the Dolphins. Alabama fans quickly

DEDICATION

Alabama fans are known as some of the most passionate in the country. In fact, the school even draws huge attendance for its A-Day Game, which is an intra-squad exhibition in the spring. In 2011, a local newspaper estimated that a record 92,310 fans showed up at Bryant-Denny Stadium for the game. It was the third time the team had drawn more than 90,000 fans for the game under Saban.

found reason to like him, though. That is because he turned the Crimson Tide back into winners.

Alabama had a 6–7 record in 2006. It moved to 7–6 in Saban's first year. However, the NCAA ruled in 2009 that Alabama again had recruiting violations and forced the Tide to forfeit 21 wins from 2005 to 2007. The upward momentum had begun, though. Alabama went 12–2 in Saban's second season. The Crimson Tide also reached the Sugar Bowl that year. The Sugar Bowl is one of five Bowl Championship Series (BCS) bowls. Only the best teams in the nation are invited to those postseason games.

CHAMPIONS AGAIN

MARK INGRAM

In 2009, Mark Ingram set the Alabama single-season record for rushing with 1,658 yards. He also caught 32 passes for 334 yards. Ingram's effort earned him the first Heisman Trophy in school history. It also helped Alabama beat Texas to win the school's thirteenth national title.

Ingram had a lot on his mind during that game against Texas. His father, also named Mark Ingram, had been an NFL wide receiver. However, he had gotten into trouble with the law. When Alabama played Texas, Ingram Sr. was in federal prison awaiting a sentence on bank fraud, money laundering, and failing to surrender on charges. That third charge came from an incident in December 2008. Ingram Sr. failed to report for a jail sentence. He wanted to watch his son, then a freshman, play in the 2009 Sugar Bowl. However, Ingram Sr. was arrested just hours before the game.

As good as the Tide were in 2008, they were even better in 2009. In fact, they were perfect. Saban led the team to a 14–0 record that year. Included was Alabama's first Southeastern Conference (SEC) title since 1999. And a few weeks after that, the top-ranked Crimson Tide beat Texas 37–21 in the BCS National Championship Game. Alabama's national title drought had finally ended.

It was a truly dominant season for the Crimson Tide. Most experts considered the SEC to be the toughest conference that season. Alabama had to beat 10 teams that would play in bowl games. One of those teams was Florida. The Gators had won two of the previous three national championships. Some consider Florida quarterback Tim Tebow to be one of the greatest college players of all time. But second-ranked Alabama rolled past top-ranked Florida 32–12 in the SEC Championship Game. That sent Alabama into the national title game against Texas.

Sophomore running back Mark Ingram led the Crimson Tide that season. In fact, he won the Heisman Trophy that year as the best player in college football. Despite Alabama's rich football history, no Crimson Tide player had won that honor before Ingram. Six Alabama players were named All-Americans during the 2009 season. It was a dramatic turnaround for the Tide.

With Saban at the helm, the success only continued. Alabama fell short of the national title game in 2010 but finished a respectable 10–3. And the Tide were again right back in the national title picture in 2011.

Alabama entered the season ranked number two in the nation. It then rolled to eight straight victories to open the year, including three over ranked opponents. That set up a game against top-ranked LSU.

Fans across the country tuned in to watch the rare regular-season game between the two top-ranked teams. Both teams had powerful defenses, and they dominated the game. Neither team was able to reach the end zone.

Each team made two field goals in regulation to tie the game at 6–6. However, Alabama's kicker missed three field goals on the day, including one in overtime. LSU eventually made an overtime field goal to win.

The Crimson Tide did not let the loss faze them. They went on to win their last three regular-season games. The LSU loss meant Alabama did not qualify for the SEC Championship Game. However, the BCS ranking system still determined that Alabama was the second-best team in the country. That led to a rematch with LSU in the BCS National Championship Game. It was the first time teams from the same conference had met for the national title since the BCS began following the 1998 season.

"GAME OF THE CENTURY"

When Alabama hosted LSU on November 5, 2011, it was a rare regular-season meeting between the first- and second-ranked teams. Those one-versus-two games are often referred to as the "Game of the Century," even though there have been several games. The 2011 game garnered a lot of excitement in SEC country. The attendance at Bryant-Denny Stadium was listed as 101,821 for the game. Several thousand more gathered outside. The fans were treated to a classic SEC-style defensive struggle. The final score of 9–6 was the second lowest in a meeting between the two top-ranked teams.

Alabama running back Trent Richardson rushes for a touchdown during the 2012 BCS title game against LSU.

The Crimson Tide treated fans to a classic SEC-style defensive performance at the championship game in New Orleans, Louisiana. Alabama's defense held LSU to only five first downs and 92 yards of total offense throughout the game. It also held the Tigers out of the end zone—and off the scoreboard entirely—in the 21–0 victory.

TRENT RICHARDSON

Alabama hardly missed a beat when 2009 Heisman Trophy-winning running back Mark Ingram left for the NFL after the 2010 season. Sophomore Trent Richardson had shined in 2010, when Ingram struggled at times with injures. Richardson rushed for 700 yards and six touchdowns that season. The Pensacola, Florida, native was even better as a junior in 2011. Richardson rushed for 1,679 yards and 21 touchdowns. He added 29 catches for 338 receiving yards and three more scores. Richardson won the Doak Walker Award as college football's best running back and finished third in voting for the Heisman Trophy. The Cleveland Browns traded up to select him third in the 2012 NFL Draft.

"That was the message before the game: to finish," Saban said after the game. "In fact, it was how bad do you want to finish? We certainly didn't play a perfect game, we got a field goal blocked, we couldn't find the end zone for a long time, but we just kept playing."

When Saban arrived at Alabama, he took over a losing team that had struggled with NCAA violations. Within five years, he brought two national titles back to Tuscaloosa, Alabama. The down period for Alabama football was officially over. And the Crimson Tide were once again one of the nation's most feared teams.

College Football Hall of Fame halfback
Millard "Dixie" Howell starred at
Alabama from 1932 to 1934.

2

THE WADE-THOMAS YEARS

THE ALABAMA FOOTBALL PROGRAM BEGAN IN 1892 UNDER COACH E. B. BEAUMONT. AS A SPORT, FOOTBALL WAS STILL VERY NEW. MANY OF TODAY'S RULES HAD NOT YET BEEN ESTABLISHED. THE SPORT'S ORGANIZATION WAS ALSO VERY DIFFERENT. AS SUCH, ALABAMA'S TEAM DID NOT PLAY VERY MANY GAMES DURING ITS EARLY SEASONS. STILL, ALABAMA HAD MOSTLY WINNING SEASONS DURING ITS EARLY YEARS.

The program began turning from good to great in 1919, when coach Xen Scott took over. He led the squad to finishes of 8–1 and 10–1 in his first two seasons. Coach Wallace Wade replaced Scott in 1923. Under Wade, the program firmly established itself as one of the nation's best.

Wade stayed at the school for only eight years. Yet in that time, the team went undefeated three times, went to its first three bowl games, and captured its first three national titles. However, two of those national titles were shared. There was no official national championship game, so various groups

FRED SINGTON

Fred Sington achieved all kinds of success while playing for coach Wallace Wade at Alabama. Sington was a 6-foot-2, 215-pound tackle. He played for the Crimson Tide from 1928 to 1930. As a senior in 1930, Sington was named an All-American.

Sington was a force on the football field. In fact, he was inducted into the College Football Hall of Fame in 1955. He was not limited to the gridiron, though. Sington earned Phi Beta Kappa honors in the classroom. That meant he earned extremely high grades. Sington also excelled in other sports. In fact, he ultimately focused most of his attention on baseball. After college, Sington played six seasons with the Washington Senators and Brooklyn Dodgers in Major League Baseball. He appeared in 181 games with a .271 batting average over his career.

named national champions after each season. In all, Wade coached the team to a 61–13–3 record.

Alabama's breakthrough came in 1925. That year, the Crimson Tide rolled through the regular season with a 9–0 record. After that, they were invited to play in their first bowl game. The Rose Bowl game in Pasadena, California, is the oldest—and many say most prestigious—bowl game. However, the Rose Bowl initially had invited Dartmouth. But the school from New Hampshire decided it was too far to travel and declined. That opened the door for Alabama.

"I put it up to the players," Wade later told *Sports Illustrated*. "Going to the Coast was a big thing. It would take us five days on a train from Tuscaloosa. I told them it would deprive them of their Christmas vacation, and that they would have to stay in training another three weeks. It took them about two minutes to make up their minds."

Still, Alabama came into the game as heavy underdogs to Washington. And the Crimson Tide fell behind by 12 points early. They did not give up, though. Alabama rallied to score 20 points in a row. Then they held off Washington to win 20–19. That gave Alabama its first national championship. It also showed that football teams from the South could compete against the best teams in the country.

Wade stayed at Alabama through the 1930 season, when he left to go to Duke. Still, Wade certainly left his mark at Alabama. The Crimson Tide also won national championships in 1926 and 1930. They later won

THE WADE-THOMAS YEARS

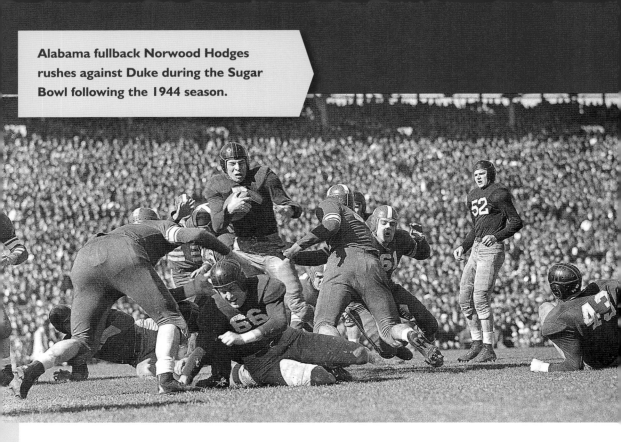

the national title outright in 1926, despite tying Stanford in the Rose
Bowl. In 1930, the Tide completed a 10–0 season with a 24–0 rout
of Washington State in the Rose Bowl. Alabama outscored opponents
271–13 that year.

Before Wade left, he was allowed to select his replacement. He
picked Frank Thomas. Thomas had played at Notre Dame under
legendary coach Knute Rockne. Then he compiled a record of 26–9–2
while coaching at Chattanooga. The Crimson Tide did not skip a beat
under the new coach. During his 15 years in charge, Alabama went 115–
24–7. The team also won two more national titles, in 1934 and 1941.

The 1934 squad went 9–0 and was invited to the school's fourth
Rose Bowl. The Crimson Tide capped off the season with a 29–13 win

over Stanford to secure Alabama's fourth national title. The Tide won another one in 1941, despite finishing 9–2. Alabama beat Texas A&M 29–21 in the Cotton Bowl to finish as national champion.

Alabama also came close to a national title in 1945. It finished 10–0 and beat the University of Southern California 34–14 in the Rose Bowl. However, voters named Army the national champion.

Playing on the 1934 team was a guy named Paul "Bear" Bryant. He would eventually become one of the most successful coaches in college football history. It was more than two decades before he would take over as head coach at Alabama.

Thomas stepped down as Alabama's coach following the 1946 season. A heart condition and high blood pressure made coaching too difficult for him. Thomas was not able to stand for extended periods. So, during his final season, he was forced to oversee many practices while riding in a trailer. Thomas was inducted into the College Football Hall of Fame in 1951.

WORLD WAR II

World War II had an effect on just about all aspects of American life during the early 1940s. College football was no exception. Alabama did not field a football team in 1943 due to the war. The Crimson Tide came back the next year, though. They went 5–2–2 and earned a berth in the Sugar Bowl. That squad was known as "The War Babies." Alabama had also sat out of the 1918 season due to World War I.

Coach Paul "Bear" Bryant compiled a
232–46–9 record while coaching Alabama
from 1958 to 1982.

3

TRULY A BEAR

ALABAMA CONTINUED TO WIN AFTER FRANK THOMAS STEPPED DOWN AS HEAD COACH. IT JUST DID NOT WIN QUITE SO MUCH FOR A WHILE. RED DREW TOOK OVER AS COACH IN 1947. THE CRIMSON TIDE HAD SEVEN WINNING SEASONS DURING HIS EIGHT YEARS IN CHARGE. HOWEVER, THEY HAD AN OVERALL RECORD OF 54–28–7 AND FELL SHORT OF ADDING ANOTHER NATIONAL TITLE.

J. B. "Ears" Whitworth took over in 1955. His first year was a disaster, as Alabama went 0–10. Through 2011, that was the only time Alabama failed to win a game and the only time Alabama lost as many as 10 games. The team only got slightly better, finishing 2–7–1 in each of the next two seasons. After that, former Alabama player and assistant coach Paul "Bear" Bryant agreed to return home.

Bryant had achieved moderate success during 15 seasons as a head coach, notably at Kentucky and Texas A&M. While at Alabama from 1958 to 1982, there was arguably no one as

successful. During his 25 seasons in charge, Bryant led the Crimson Tide to a 232–46–9 record. Included in that were six national titles. Alabama also went to a bowl game after every season except the first one under Bryant. He became one of the country's most famous and most respected coaches.

"Even his peers in the coaching business felt in awe of him," said former Penn State coach Joe Paterno, who ended his career with more wins than any other coach. "He had such charisma. He was just a giant figure."

Bryant had a gravelly voice and a tough way about him as he roamed the sidelines in his signature houndstooth hat. He got the nickname "Bear" from something that happened when he was a boy.

At age 13, Bryant was already 6-foot-1 and weighed 180 pounds. One day, somebody offered him $1 to wrestle a bear at a local carnival. Bryant took the offer. The bear ended up biting Bryant on the ear. Bryant never did get his money from the carnival, but the nickname stayed with him forever.

"His nickname was Bear," said Hall of Fame quarterback Joe Namath, who played for Bryant at Alabama from 1962 to 1964. "Now imagine a guy that can carry the nickname Bear."

Bryant was a no-nonsense, hard-working person. He demanded his players give their best all the time. He would not settle for anything less. If a player did not play as hard as possible, he would not get much time on the field.

"I'M GOING HOME"

Paul "Bear" Bryant was coaching Texas A&M when Alabama called in 1958. The Crimson Tide wanted him to coach the football team and be the school's athletic director. Bryant signed a 10-year contract. Afterward, he addressed his Texas A&M players. "I've heard Mama calling, and now I'm going home," Bryant famously told them.

Bryant quickly made his presence known in Tuscaloosa. He stopped there to visit with his new team on the way to Florida for the Gator Bowl. Bryant called for a 1:15 p.m. meeting. One of Alabama's top players showed up late. The door had already been locked. Bryant would not open it.

"Go see who that is," Bryant reportedly said. "And tell him, whoever it is, that we don't need him."

The Crimson Tide went only 5–4–1 in Bryant's first year. But they quickly improved. Alabama went to 24 consecutive bowl games under Bryant beginning in 1959.

TRULY A BEAR

"I don't want ordinary people," Bryant once said. "I want people who are willing to sacrifice and do without a lot of those things ordinary students get to do. That's what it takes to win."

Bryant proved over his 25 seasons in Tuscaloosa that he knew how to coach a winning football team. Alabama suffered through three of its worst seasons before Bryant took over as head coach. Everything changed after that.

The Crimson Tide again began to play strong defense. Even though the offense still struggled, things were turning around for the team. Alabama gave up 173 points in a 2–7–1 finish in 1957 under Whitworth. The Crimson Tide allowed just 75 points during Bryant's first season in 1958. They did not give up more than 14 points in any game that season. Alabama improved to 5–4–1 in Bryant's first season. That is far from a national championship. But it was a big improvement over Alabama's 2–7–1 mark in each of the previous two seasons.

THE JUNCTION BOYS

In later years, Bear Bryant again became known thanks to Jim Dent's book titled *The Junction Boys*. That book was later made into a very successful movie. It was about how hard Bryant drove his first team at Texas A&M in 1954. The players were going through their training camp in very hot conditions. Approximately 111 players began the workout. Only 35 finished. The team was known as "The Junction Boys" because its training camp was held in the town of Junction, Texas.

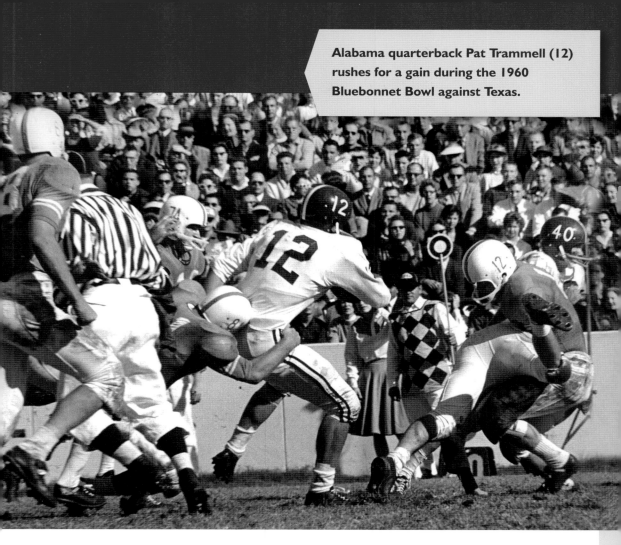

The defense got even better the next season, in 1959. Alabama then gave up only 59 points. The Crimson Tide allowed 17 points in a season-opening loss to Georgia. Alabama never gave up more than seven points the rest of the year. The team finished 7–2–2 and was invited to the Liberty Bowl. It was Alabama's first bowl game since 1953.

After just two seasons with Bryant, Alabama was clearly back on the right track. And it would only get better in the 1960s.

TRULY A BEAR

Alabama coach Bear Bryant talks with quarterback Joe Namath during the 1964 season.

A SUCCESSFUL BEAR

THE 1960S BELONGED TO BEAR BRYANT AND HIS FOOTBALL TEAM. ALABAMA WON THREE NATIONAL TITLES AND FOUR SEC TITLES DURING THE DECADE. THE CRIMSON TIDE WERE DOMINANT, ESPECIALLY IN THE FIRST PART OF THE DECADE. THEY WON THEIR NATIONAL TITLES WITH RECORDS OF 11–0 (1961), 10–1 (1964), AND 9–1–1 (1965).

Bryant had no problem disciplining his best players, including star quarterbacks Joe Namath and Kenny Stabler. Bryant suspended Namath late in the 1963 season, which cost Namath a trip to the Sugar Bowl. The coach put Namath back on the roster the following year, and the Tide went on to win the national title.

Namath was known as someone who enjoyed going to parties. Stabler behaved in a similar way when he arrived at Alabama in 1964. He got several speeding tickets, skipped football and baseball practice, and at times cut class. As a junior in 1966, Stabler led the Crimson Tide to an 11–0 record.

However, the team did not earn the national championship votes that year. Bryant said in several places that this actually might have been his best team ever, even though it came up short of a title. Keith Dunnavant's book *The Missing Ring* talked about how the Crimson Tide lost the national title despite the perfect season.

Even with Stabler's success, the coach finally grew sick of Stabler's antics during the spring of 1967. Bryant sent Stabler a telegram that read: "You have been indefinitely suspended. —Coach Paul W. Bryant." Namath then sent Stabler a telegram the following day, which simply read: "He means it."

"The last few months, Ken [Stabler] has been disregarding these regulations and conforming to his own or those set up by someone else," Bryant said at the time. "The other members of the squad conform quite well and willingly."

Stabler finally got his act together after that. Bryant let Stabler back on the team. However, the star quarterback needed to work his way back from the bottom of the depth chart in spring practices. Stabler

LEE ROY JORDAN

Linebacker Lee Roy Jordan was one of Alabama's top defensive players under coach Bear Bryant. After Alabama went 9–1 during the 1962 regular season, the Crimson Tide earned a berth in the Orange Bowl. Jordan truly was all over the field that day. He made 31 tackles in Alabama's 17–0 win over Oklahoma. Jordan went on to be a very good linebacker in the NFL.

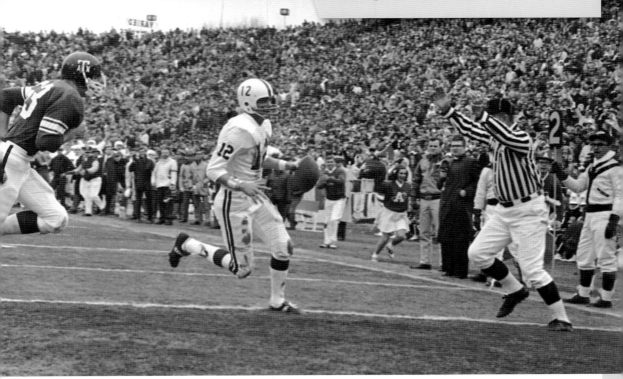

eventually won back the starting job, and he was always grateful to Bryant for pushing him so hard.

"I was young and dumb and making bad decisions," Stabler said many years later. "[I was] not doing what I needed to be doing, but Coach Bryant saw something worth saving and let me know all that I was throwing away. Without Coach Bryant, who knows where I'd be."

The Crimson Tide slipped a bit later in the decade. They went 6–5 in 1969 and 6–5–1 the following year. Bryant turned it around after that, though. He brought back the strong defense that helped him change things when he first arrived at Alabama.

In 1971, the Crimson Tide bounced back to win the SEC title. The defense allowed 10 points or less nine times that season. However, after going 11–0 in the regular season, the Tide lost 38–6 to Nebraska in that season's Orange Bowl.

Still, Alabama was again on its way. The Tide won the national title three times in that decade. It took the championship in 1973, 1978, and 1979. The 1978 national title matchup was against Penn State. The Tide edged Penn State 14–7 after a famous goal-line stand in the Sugar Bowl.

Bryant's health started to fade after that season. The Tide remained successful, but questions kept coming up about how long Bryant would coach. That uncertainty appeared to hurt Alabama's recruiting.

Bryant's career—and life—then came to a sad ending. He surprised many with his decision to resign as Alabama's coach following the 1982 season. The Crimson Tide made the Liberty Bowl that year and edged Illinois 21–15. That would be Bryant's final game.

WISHBONE OFFENSE

Texas coach Darrell Royal created the wishbone offense in 1968 to take advantage of his star running backs. The wishbone involved a fullback lining up in front of two running backs. That made it very hard for the defense to figure out blocking schemes and who had the ball. In 1971, Bryant went to Royal to learn how to run the wishbone. The new offense helped Alabama get back on track after a few mediocre seasons.

Alabama's star tight end Ozzie Newsome runs with the ball during a 1974 game at Miami.

Bryant died four weeks later. He had been having health problems in the years before that. The years of high-pressure strain apparently just wore him down.

"He literally coached himself to death," said then-Ohio State coach Woody Hayes at Bryant's funeral. "He was our greatest coach."

Even decades after Bryant's death, many still agree with Hayes that Bryant was the greatest football coach of all time. His 323 career victories (232 of them at Alabama) broke the previous record set by

BARRY KRAUSS

Linebacker Barry Krauss starred for the Crimson Tide from 1976 to 1978. As a sophomore, he was named Most Valuable Player (MVP) of the 1976 Liberty Bowl. However, fans remember him the most for the famous "Goal-line Stand" game in the Sugar Bowl following the 1978 season. With time running out, Penn State had a first-and-goal on Alabama's 8-yard line. After three plays, Penn State was still short of the end zone. Then on the fourth play, Krauss made the crucial tackle on Penn State fullback Mike Guman. The stop helped Alabama seal the 14–7 win. And the All-American linebacker was named Sugar Bowl MVP.

The Baltimore Colts picked Krauss in the first round of the 1979 NFL Draft. Krauss had 10 successful seasons with the Colts and one with the Miami Dolphins. Krauss now works as a broadcaster and speaker. He remains very popular with Alabama fans.

Amos Alonzo Stagg. His teams never had a losing record, and they went to bowl games in 24 consecutive seasons. They also won national championships in 1961, 1964, 1965, 1973, 1978, and 1979 before he stepped down.

Bryant was well-known for his hard-driving ways. He loved football and lived for coaching it. In a 1979 interview with *People* magazine, Bryant talked about how hard he pushed himself, even at the age of 66.

Bryant would wake up at 5 a.m. and find his way to work 30 minutes later. He would then remain at his office until eight or nine o'clock at night. A friend of Bryant's said that he "used to work 22 hours a day. Now he only works 19." The reason he worked so much was that he loved his job and enjoyed the sport.

"People always ask 'what is it like to play for Coach Bryant?'" Stabler said. "We would play teams that were always bigger, always faster, always more of them—and we always won.

That was because of Coach Bryant. He outcoached the other guy. He out-motivated the other guy."

Although Bryant worked his players hard, they missed his guidance. In *The Missing Ring*, former Alabama running back Ed Morgan talked about Bryant's willingness to give a hand to his players long after their football careers were done. "People just don't understand how much Coach Bryant did for people after they quit playing for him," Morgan said. "All you had to do was work hard and keep your nose clean, and he was always there for you."

A SUCCESSFUL BEAR

Alabama linebacker Keith McCants was a consensus All-American as a senior in 1989.

SABAN BRINGS SUCCESS

ALABAMA WAS ONE OF THE UNDISPUTED POWERS OF COLLEGE FOOTBALL FOR A QUARTER OF A CENTURY UNDER BEAR BRYANT. LIFE AFTER THE LEGENDARY COACH PROVED TO BE DIFFICULT AT TIMES.

Alabama fans wanted national championships. Ray Perkins, who took over after Bryant, fell short of that. In 1984, Alabama went 5–6. It was the team's first losing season since 1957. Although Perkins rebounded to lead Alabama to 9–2–1 and 10–3 seasons, the school replaced him after the 1986 season.

Bill Curry then coached the team to the SEC title in 1989. That was the first time the Tide had won the conference title since 1981. Then he surprised many by leaving to coach Kentucky before the 1990 season. Curry said he was tired of the pressure that came with the Crimson Tide job. Curry knew about pressure. He had played on NFL championship

teams as a lineman for the Baltimore Colts and Green Bay Packers. He had competed at the highest levels. But coaching at Alabama turned out to be something different and difficult.

His wife, Carolyn Curry, talked about that pressure in a January 1990 Associated Press story. She said that "every time we lose one game here, they start talking about firing your husband. That's what makes it different at Alabama."

Gene Stallings, one of Bryant's "Junction Boys," took over after that. Stallings had coached in both college and professional football. He understood how important football was to those in Alabama. Although the Crimson Tide had been above average under Perkins and Curry, they finally rose back to the top under Stallings.

The Tide jumped from 7–5 in his first season to 11–1 in his second season. Then in 1992, Alabama went 13–0 and won its first national title since 1979. Talking about his success at Alabama in a 2006 interview, Stallings displayed a very simple formula for winning games.

"You win football games with football players making plays," he said. "If you have good players and they stay healthy, you can have a successful team. It's about the execution."

Alabama remained a top team under Stallings. But things began to fall apart once he left, following the 1996 season.

THE IRON BOWL

The Iron Bowl between Alabama and Auburn is one of the most anticipated college football games each season. The bitter rivals are located just 160 miles (257 km) apart, and both teams are often among the best in the nation. However, the rivalry is intense even during down seasons. After all, in-state bragging rights are on the line.

Auburn and Alabama first played each other in 1893. However, the Iron Bowl did not become an annual game until 1948. The game used to be held in neutral Birmingham, Alabama. Although Auburn had played twice at Alabama in 1895 and 1901, Alabama did not play a game at Auburn until 1989. Since 1999 the Iron Bowl has rotated between Auburn and Alabama's campuses.

Through 2011, Alabama held a 39–34–1 advantage in the all-time series. But Auburn has held the advantage in the modern era. The Tigers won eight of the 12 games from 2000 to 2011.

SABAN BRINGS SUCCESS

Mike DuBose took over and went just 24–23 during his four years. Then, Dennis Franchione went 17–8 over two seasons before he suddenly left to coach at Texas A&M late in 2002. The move upset many at Alabama. The coach was reportedly uncomfortable with the fact that the Tide would again be facing NCAA punishments in the following year.

Mike Shula replaced Franchione in 2003. Shula had been an Alabama quarterback, and his father was a Hall of Fame coach in the NFL.

The Tide struggled, though. They went 4–9 in Shula's first season. Although they won 10 games in 2005, Shula was fired as the Tide struggled through another losing season in 2006.

Alabama fans were used to success. Princeton and Yale had each won more than 20 national titles during college football's earliest years. Outside of them, however, no school had won more national titles than Alabama's 12. Michigan and Notre Dame were next with 11. However, in the years after Stallings left, the Tide never came very close to winning number 13. Part of that was due to NCAA sanctions. Alabama had violated recruiting rules during the 1990s, so the NCAA took away scholarships and barred the Tide from the 2002 and 2003 postseasons.

Alabama athletic director Mal Moore decided Alabama needed a major change in the culture around the football team. So in 2007, he hired Nick Saban, a proven but sometimes controversial coach who had led LSU to a national title.

Saban had won everywhere he had been. The problem was that he had been a lot of places. Because of that, people did not always trust him.

SET IN STONE

Every Alabama coach who has won a national championship has a statue in front of Bryant-Denny Stadium, where the Tide plays its home games. After Alabama won the 2009 title, coach Nick Saban's likeness joined those of Bear Bryant, Gene Stallings, Frank Thomas, and Wallace Wade.

SABAN BRINGS SUCCESS

When Saban agreed to take the Alabama offer, it upset a lot of people in Miami. That is because he already had a very good contract with the NFL's Dolphins. But he still suddenly took the job at Alabama.

Saban also faced a difficult task upon his arrival at Alabama. The team was just 26–23 under Shula with a losing record of 13–19 in the SEC and a 2–14 record against rivals Arkansas, Auburn, LSU, and Tennessee.

Alabama had some growing pains in Saban's first year. Louisiana-Monroe stunned the Tide at home 21–14 late in the season. After the game, Saban told his team that good things sometimes come from bad situations. And that is what happened. The Tide improved the next year, and they went on to win the national title the following season in 2009. Alabama finished 10–3 with a win in the Capital One Bowl in 2010 before making it back to the top in 2011.

The defense, like it had under Bryant, shined in 2011. Alabama gave up only nine offensive touchdowns in 13 games. The highlight was the 21–0 win over LSU in the BCS National Championship Game.

RUN STOPPERS

Alabama was strong all over in 2009 en route to a program-record 14 wins and its thirteenth national title. The Crimson Tide were particularly strong on defense. Following the national title win, Alabama's defense had not allowed for a 100-plus-yard rusher in 34 games. The last running back to do that against Alabama was in October 2007. Only one team allowed fewer than Alabama's 11.71 points per game in 2009. The strong defensive tradition at Alabama lived on.

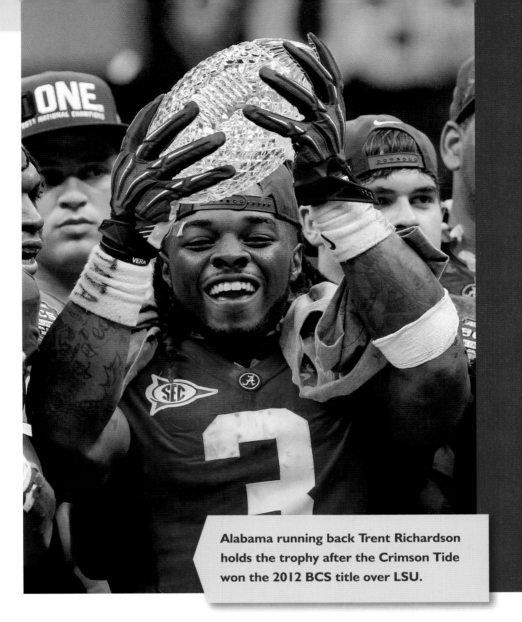

Alabama running back Trent Richardson holds the trophy after the Crimson Tide won the 2012 BCS title over LSU.

Alabama's defense was so good that night that LSU could not even get across midfield until about eight minutes were left in the fourth quarter. That is the kind of domination Alabama fans became used to over the years under coaches Bryant, Wallace Wade, Frank Thomas, Saban, and others. And the Crimson Tide showed no signs of slowing down.

[41]

TIMELINE

Alabama plays its first football game.

Alabama wraps up its first national championship by upsetting Washington 20–19 in the Rose Bowl on January 1, 1926.

Coach Wallace Wade announces he is leaving Alabama at season's end to go coach at Duke. Still, the Tide wins their third national title before he goes.

Coach Frank Thomas steps down following the season due to health problems. The Tide won two national titles under him, in 1934 and 1941.

Paul "Bear" Bryant takes over as coach and immediately turns around the program.

1892 1925 1930 1946 1958

Alabama wins the national title when it edges Penn State 14–7 in the Sugar Bowl. The famed "Goal-line Stand" helps the Tide hold off the Nittany Lions.

Alabama wins its sixth and final national title under Bryant.

Bryant decides to retire after the 1982 season. He dies unexpectedly four weeks later. Former Alabama player Ray Perkins steps in as the new coach in 1983.

Bill Curry takes over as coach in a hiring that causes some controversy among Alabama fans.

Coach Gene Stallings leads Alabama to the school's twelfth national championship, completing a perfect season.

1978 1979 1982 1987 1992

Alabama wins its first national championship under Bryant, finishing with an 11–0 record.

Despite losing to Texas 21–17 in the Orange Bowl, Alabama still wins a national title.

Alabama comes into the Orange Bowl ranked number four, wins that game, and moves to number one to claim the national title after the top three teams lose.

Alabama goes undefeated but does not take the national title.

Searching for something to make his offense perform better, Bryant installs the wishbone formation.

1961 1964 1965 1966 1971

The Tide go just 4–7 under new coach Mike DuBose. It is their first losing season in 13 years.

The NCAA gives Alabama a two-year ban from bowl games for various recruiting violations.

Nick Saban leaves the Miami Dolphins to become Alabama's head coach.

Alabama wins its thirteenth national title overall with a 37–21 win over Texas in the BCS title game on January 7.

Alabama wins another national title after a dominant 21–0 victory over LSU in the BCS title game on January 9.

1997 2002 2007 2010 2012

QUICK STATS

PROGRAM INFO
University of Alabama Cadets,
   Crimson White (1892–1906)
University of Alabama
   Crimson Tide (1907–)

NATIONAL CHAMPIONSHIPS
(* DENOTES SHARED TITLE)
1925, 1926*, 1930*, 1934*, 1941*, 1961,
1964, 1965*, 1973*, 1978*, 1979, 1992,
2009, 2011

OTHER ACHIEVEMENTS
BCS bowl appearances (1999–): 4
SEC championships (1933–): 22
Bowl record: 34–22–3

HEISMAN TROPHY WINNERS
Mark Ingram, 2009

KEY PLAYERS
(POSITION[S]; SEASONS WITH TEAM)
Shaun Alexander (RB; 1996–99)
John Hannah (OL; 1970–72)
Don Hutson, (WR; 1932–34)
Mark Ingram (RB; 2008–10)
Lee Roy Jordan (C/LB; 1960–62)

* All statistics through 2011 season

Joe Namath (QB; 1962–64)
Ozzie Newsome (TE; 1974–77)
Fred Sington (T; 1928–30)
Kenny Stabler (QB; 1965–67)
Bart Starr (QB; 1953–55)
Derrick Thomas (LB; 1985–88)

KEY COACHES
Paul "Bear" Bryant (1958–82):
   232–46–9; 12–10–2 (bowl games)
Nick Saban (2007–):
   50–12; 4–1 (bowl games)
Wallace Wade (1923–30):
   61–13–3; 2–0–1 (bowl games)

HOME STADIUM
Bryant-Denny Stadium (1929–)

Apparently, the unusual name "Crimson Tide" actually came from Hugh Roberts, who was a sports editor at the *Birmingham Age-Herald*. He wrote the term when talking about what happened in the Alabama-Auburn football game of 1907. It was a very muddy day—with lots of red mud—and other writers in the area began using the term as well.

"If you had told me two years ago we'd be here today, I'd have called you a liar." —Alabama quarterback Greg McElroy after the Tide beat Texas 37–21 in the BCS National Championship Game for the 2009 season

Paul "Bear" Bryant stepped down as Alabama's coach at the end of the 1982 season. He then died suddenly in early January 1983, just four weeks later. The Alabama football program decided to honor him in a small way. The players wore stickers with his famous houndstooth hat on their helmets during that next season as a tribute. Many people who know about Alabama football recognize that hat, even today, many years later.

"I ain't never been nothing but a winner." —Long-time Alabama head coach Bear Bryant, describing the success he had during his career with the Crimson Tide and other places.

GLOSSARY

All-American
A player chosen as one of the best amateurs in the country in a particular activity.

athletic director
An administrator who oversees the coaches, players, and teams of an institution.

conference
In sports, a group of teams that plays each other each season.

draft
A system used by professional sports leagues to select new players in order to spread incoming talent among all teams. The NFL Draft is held each spring.

momentum
A continued strong performance based on recent success.

motivated
Caused someone to do well.

recruiting
Trying to entice a player to come to a certain school.

rivals
Opponents that bring out great emotion in a team, its fans, and its players.

roster
The players on a football team.

sanctions
The penalties a football program gets after breaking NCAA rules.

scholarship
Financial assistance awarded to students to help them pay for school. Top athletes earn scholarships to represent a college through its sports teams.

upset
A result where the supposedly worse team defeats the supposedly better team.

FOR MORE INFORMATION

FURTHER READING

Dunnavant, Keith. *The Missing Ring: How Bear Bryant and the 1966 Alabama Crimson Tide Were Denied College Football's Most Elusive Prize.* New York: Thomas Dunne Books, 2006.

Keith, Don. *The Bear: The Legendary Life of Coach Paul "Bear" Bryant.* Nashville, TN: Cumberland House, 2006.

Sharpe, Wilton. *Crimson Tide Madness: Great Eras in Alabama Football.* Nashville, TN: Cumberland House, 2007.

WEB LINKS

To learn more about the Alabama Crimson Tide, visit ABDO Publishing Company online at **www.abdopublishing.com.** Web sites about the Crimson Tide are featured on our Book Links page. These links are routinely monitored and updated to provide the most current information available.

PLACES TO VISIT

Bryant-Denny Stadium
920 Paul W. Bryant Drive
Tuscaloosa, AL 35401
(205) 348-3600
http://tour.ua.edu/tourstops/bryantdenny. html

This has been Alabama's home field since 1929.

College Football Hall of Fame
111 South St. Joseph St.
South Bend, IN 46601
1-800-440-FAME (3263)
www.collegefootball.org

This hall of fame and museum highlights the greatest players and moments in the history of college football. Among the former Alabama players enshrined here are Lee Roy Jordan, Fred Sington, and coach Paul "Bear" Bryant.

Paul W. Bryant Museum
300 Paul W. Bryant Drive
Tuscaloosa, AL 35487
(866) 772-BEAR (2327) or
(205) 348-4668
www.bryantmuseum.com

This museum is all about Bear Bryant and Crimson Tide football.

INDEX

ABOUT THE AUTHOR

Jeff Seidel has been a sportswriter for 25 years in the Baltimore-Washington area. He has written three books and lives in Baltimore with his wife, two children, and two cats.